Antarctic Animals

Alan Trussell-Cullen

Australia • Brazil • Japan • Korea • Mexico • Singapore • Spain • United Kingdom • United States

Antarctic Animals

Fast Forward
Blue Level 9

Text: Alan Trussell-Cullen
Illustrations: Boris Silvestri
Editor: Kate McGough
Design: Vonda Pestana
Series design: James Lowe
Production controller: Emma Hayes
Photo research: Corrina Tauschke
Audio recordings: Juliet Hill, Picture Start
Spoken by: Matthew King and Abbe Holmes
Reprint: Jennifer Foo

Acknowledgements
The author and publisher would like to acknowledge permission to reproduce material from the following sources: Photographs by National Science Foundation/Jaime Ramos, pp 3, 8/Photolibrary.com/Peter Arnold Images Inc, cover, pp 1, 5/BAS, p14/Roland Birke, p9/DAL, pp 5 inset, 15 top/Oxford Scientific Films, pp 7 bottom, 13/Science Photo Library, p4/Photolibrary.com/AGE Fotostock/Fritz Poelking, p7 top/Photolibrary.com/Animals Animals/OSF/Osborne, Ben, p15 bottom/Photolibrary.com/Science Photo Library/Doug Allen, back cover, p6.

ISBN 978 0 17 012532 1
ISBN 978 0 17 012525 3 (set)

Cengage Learning Australia
Level 7, 80 Dorcas Street
South Melbourne, Victoria Australia 3205
Phone: 1300 790 853

Cengage Learning New Zealand
Unit 4B Rosedale Office Park
331 Rosedale Road, Albany, North Shore NZ 0632
Phone: 0508 635 766

For learning solutions, visit cengage.com.au

Printed in Australia by Ligare Pty Ltd
9 10 11 12 13 14 15 22 21 20 19 18

THE UNIVERSITY OF
MELBOURNE

Evaluated in independent research by staff from the Department of Language, Literacy and Arts Education at the University of Melbourne.

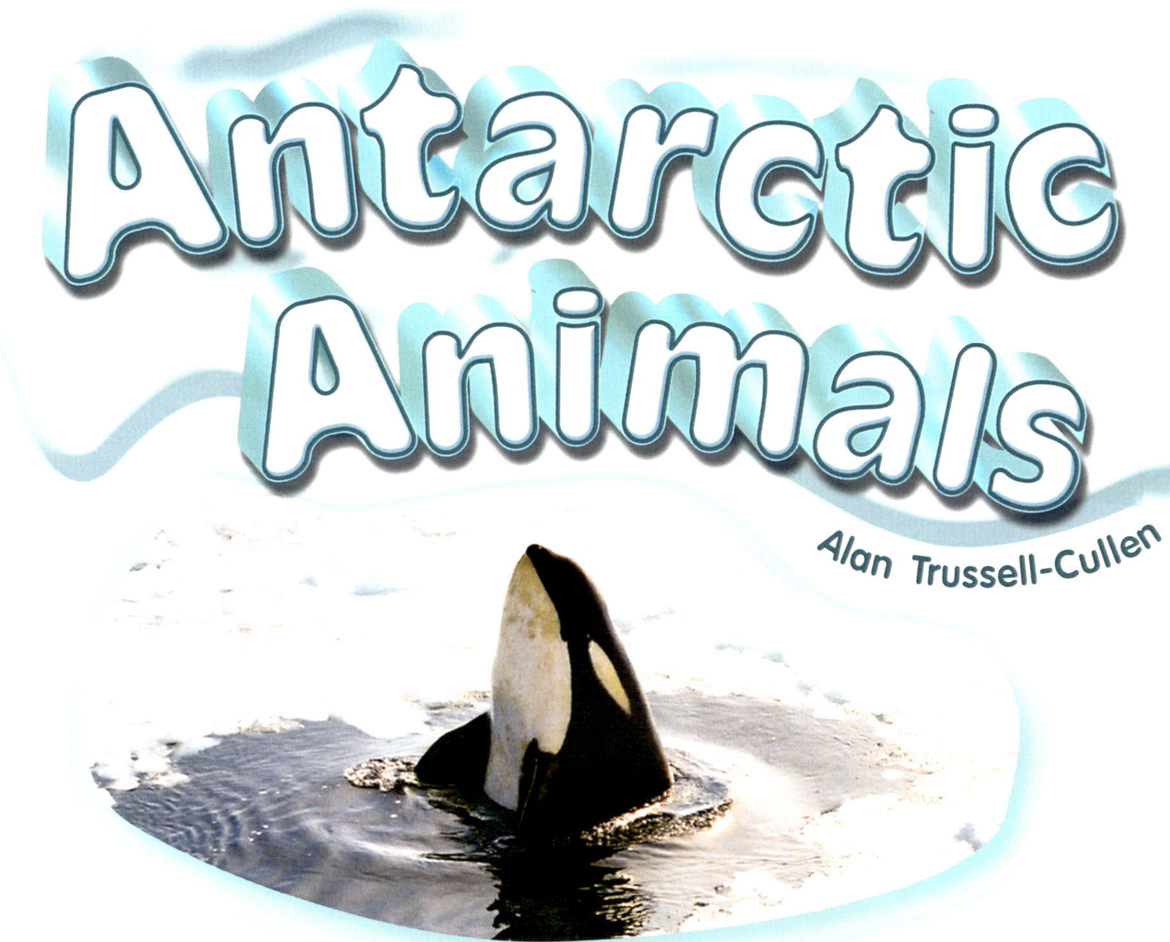

Antarctic Animals

Alan Trussell-Cullen

Contents

Chapter 1

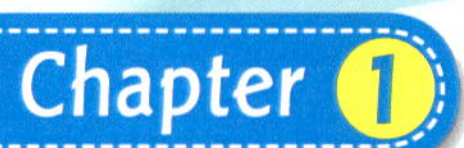

The Coldest Place on Earth

Antarctica is one of the coldest places on Earth.

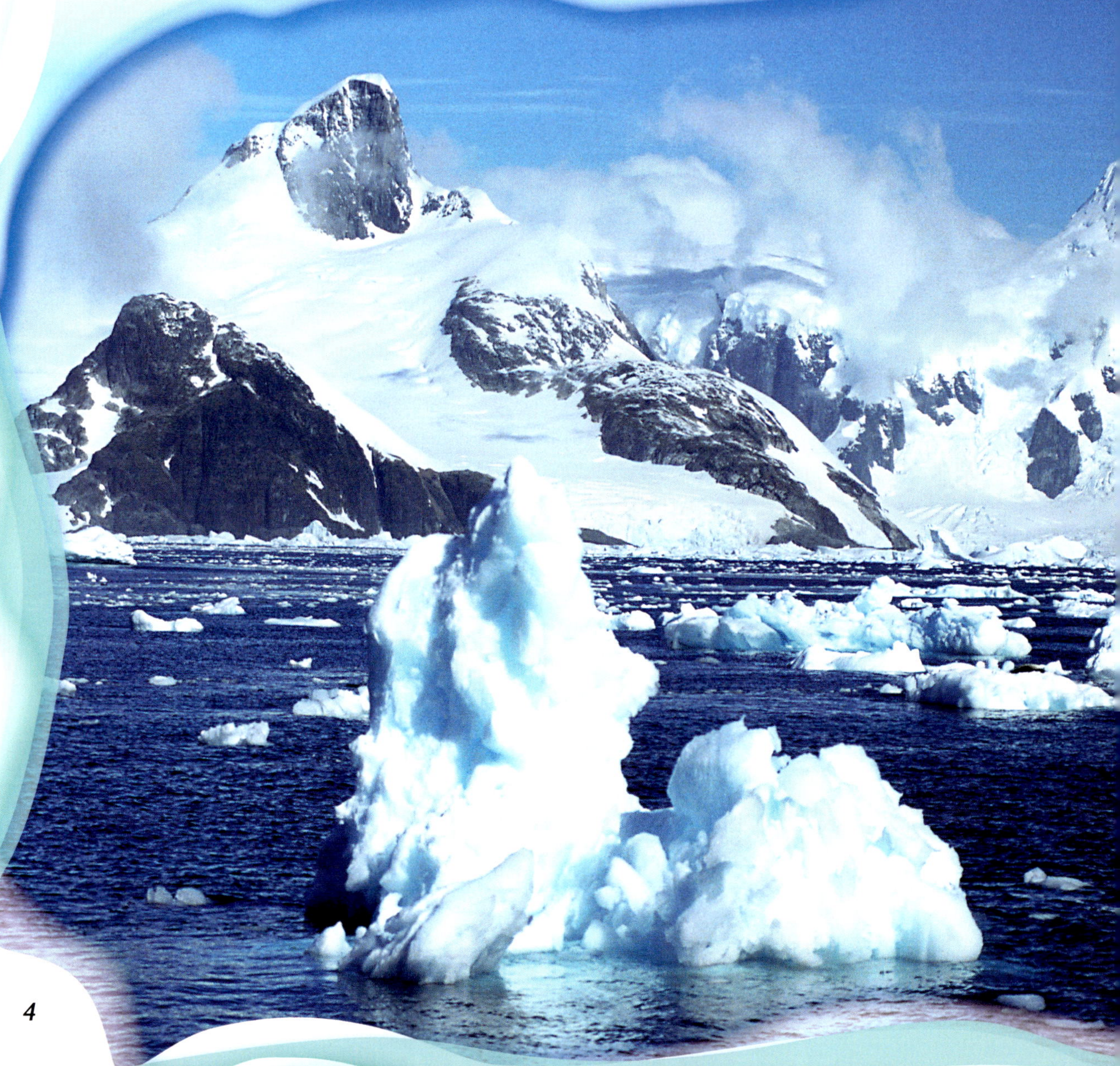

There is ice over most of the land.
There is also ice over the sea.
But many animals and plants live there.

Chapter 2

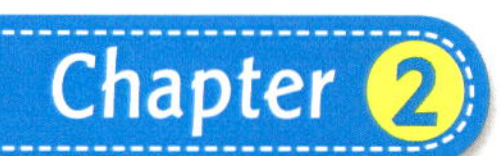

Keeping Out the Cold

All animals that live in Antarctica
have ways to keep out the cold.

Seals have layers of fat
that help keep out the cold
as they swim under the ice, looking for food.

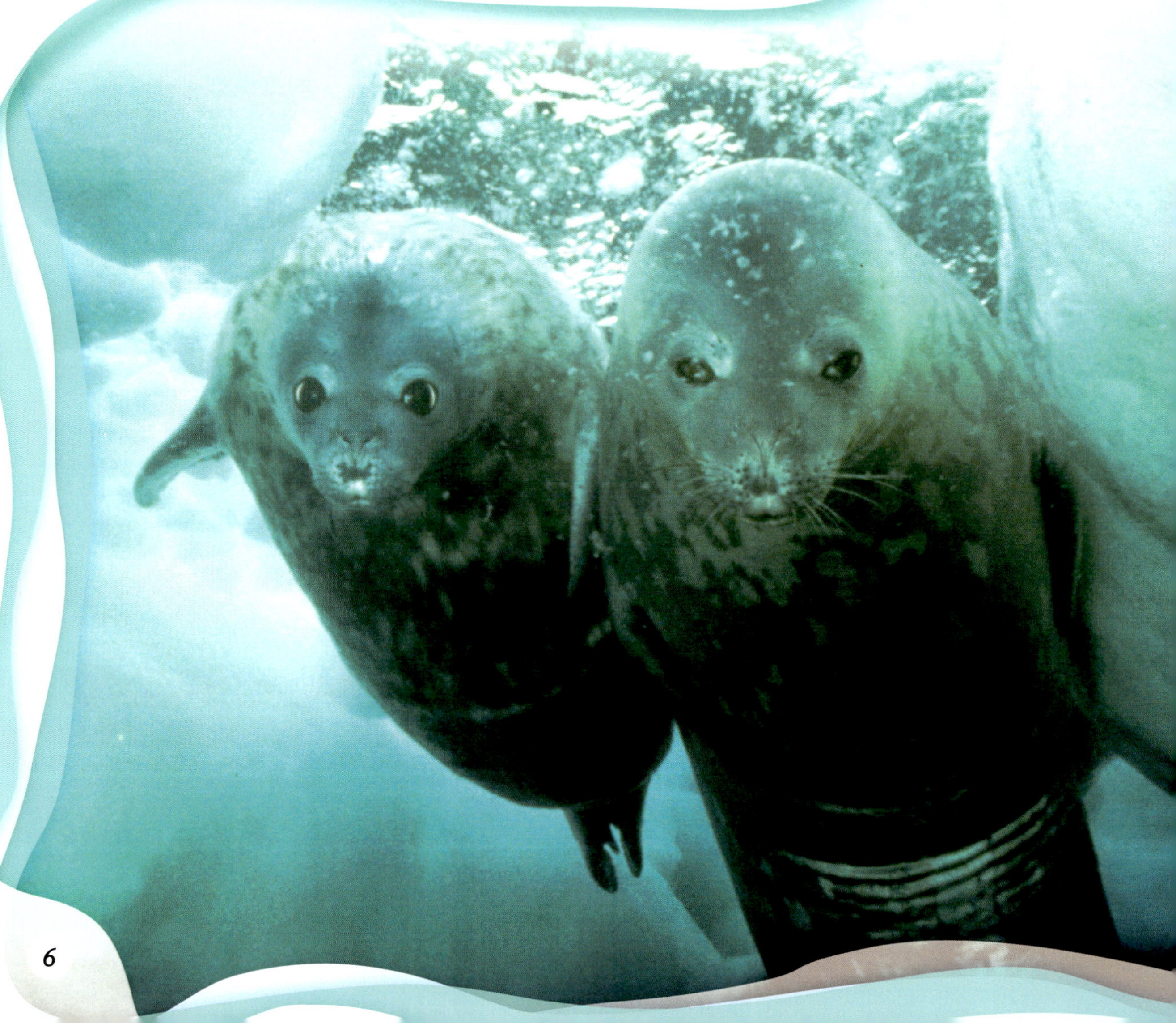

Penguins have thick layers of feathers that keep out the cold.

Penguins cannot fly, but they can swim well.

Chapter 3

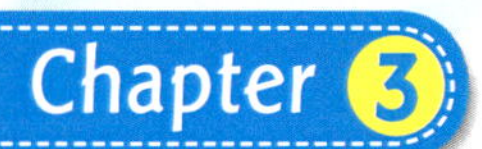

Life in the Water

Plants and animals need **oxygen** to live.
Sea plants and many sea animals
get their oxygen from the water.

Cold water holds a lot of oxygen,
so many plants and animals
live and feed
in the cold Antarctic sea.

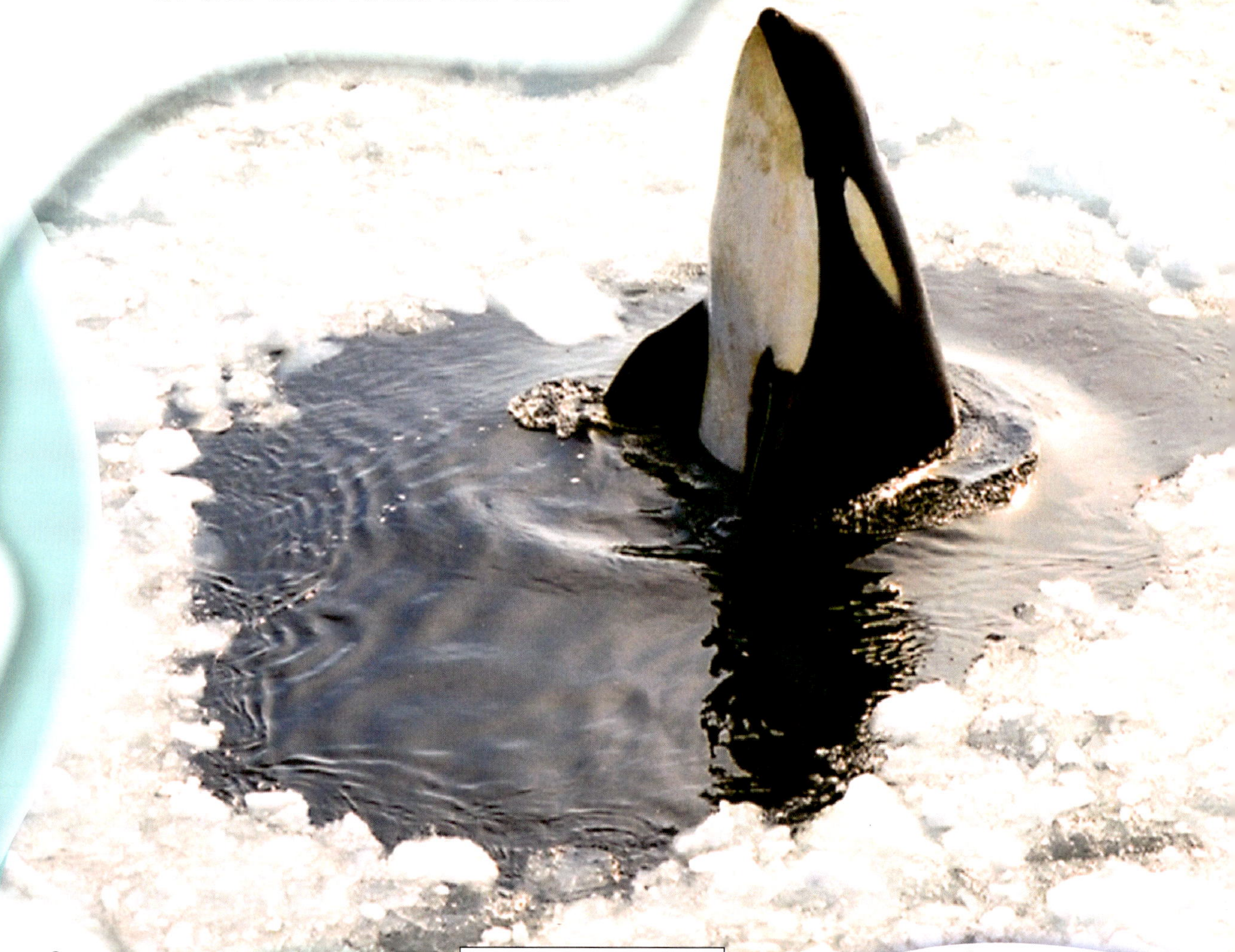

Running Words 122

Some of these plants and animals
are so little
that they are hard to see.
They are called plankton.

Plankton are a mix of plants and animals.

Chapter 4

The Food Chain

All the animals that live in Antarctica need one another for food.

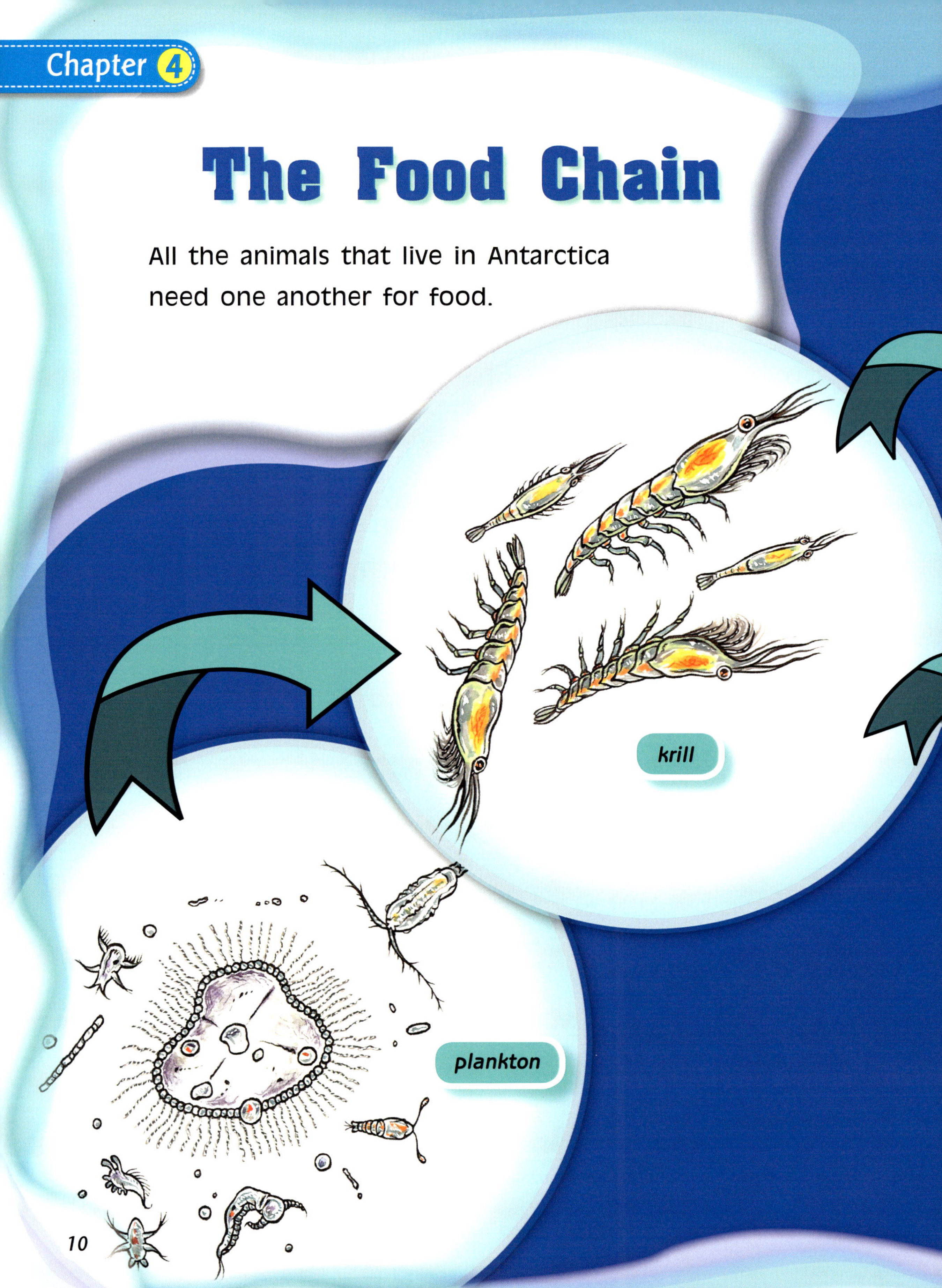

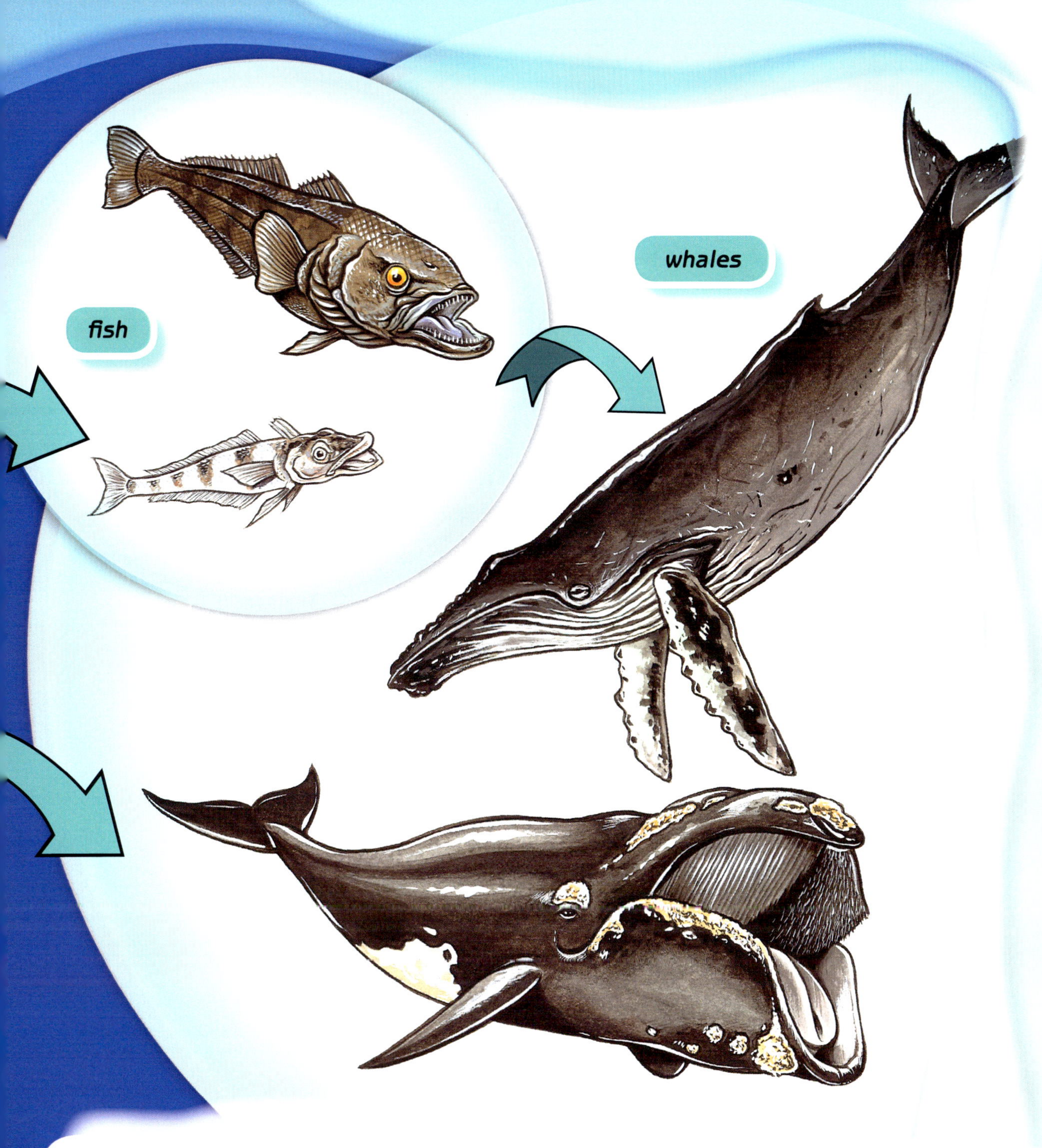

Plankton is the start of the Antarctic **food chain**.
Krill eat the plankton.
Fish and whales come to Antarctic waters
to eat the krill.

Many seals eat the fish.
Seabirds also feed on the fish in Antarctic waters.

But there is a new part to the food chain – people.
People also go to Antarctic waters to catch fish.
Every year, they catch more fish than the year before.

Looking after Antarctica

Scientists go to Antarctica
to find out all they can
about the animals that live there.

Scientists believe that fishing in Antarctic waters
will change the animals' lives.
They think that too many people are going to Antarctica
and taking too many fish.

The animals that eat the fish
may not find food to eat.
This may change the food chain.
Then everything in the food chain
will change forever.

Glossary

food chain how plants and animals depend on one another for food

oxygen a gas in the air. All living things need oxygen.

scientists people who study and learn about the world around us

Index